ANIMAL ANTIPODES

Carly Allen-Fletcher

AN • ti • poad (s.)

an • TI • peh • deez (pl.)

Earth, your home.

A world full of wonderful
places, each as unique as the
animals that live there.

Everywhere on Earth has an ANTIPODE —
a place directly opposite it on the other
side of the globe.

Icy mountains, dry deserts, and tropical
seas, no matter how different, have one
thing in common — they are home to all
kinds of amazing animals.

Each creature has evolved and
adapted to live in their own special
place in the world.

Let's explore some antipodes
and find out which animals,
big and small, fast and slow,
are opposites on Earth.

The North Pole. Under the northern lights, polar bears roam by icy waves. Their thick waterproof fur keeps them warm in the freezing cold.

The North Pole is the antipode to...

The South Pole. In the seas around the South Pole, penguins dive for fish. Their fat layer of blubber protects them from the icy water.

The Okavango Delta, Botswana. African elephants keep cool by wading in the mud of the swamps. The mud helps to keep the insects away, too.

The Okavango Delta is the antipode to...

The Big Island, Hawaii. Around the many volcanic islands of Hawaii, turtles crawl out of the ocean to bask on the warm sands.

Desert National Park, India. Antelope race across the sandy dunes of this giant nature reserve. They have to be fast to outrun hungry wolves.
Desert National Park is the antipode of...

Easter Island. This remote island in the Pacific Ocean is home to mysterious statues, wild horses, and many squawking seabirds.

Palembang, Indonesia. Thousands of belida fish glide through cool waters by this riverside city, hoping to avoid the local fishermen.

Palembang is the antipode of...

La Jagua, Huila, Colombia. Lizards lounge by the dusty roads of this quiet town. Their rock-colored scales help them hide from dangerous birds of prey.

Kaoh Nheaek, Cambodia. These giant jungles are home to a variety of snakes. They slither through the rivers and high branches at night, searching for tasty birds' eggs. Kaoh Nheaek is the antipode to...

Machu Picchu, Peru. High on a mountain in South America, llamas wander through the ruins of this Inca settlement.

Lake Baikal, Siberia. The biggest freshwater lake in the world is the home of Baikal seals. Thousands of plants and animals share the cold, deep waters.

Lake Baikal is the antipode to...

Monte Sarmiento, Chile. This towering mountain is a tough place to survive. Foxes creep around its snowy sides in search of rabbits.

Xi'an, China. Forested mountains and valleys surround this ancient city. Pandas laze around, eating bamboo all day.

Xi'an, China is the antipode to...

Santiago, Chile. This sprawling city lies on a vast, flat plain.
High above, condors glide in search of carrion.

Hong Kong. The shining skyscrapers and high-rise hotels of this city have some special guests. At night, tiny bats leave their hidden homes and flutter across the sky.

Hong Kong is the antipode of...

La Quiaca, Argentina. Peaceful plains surround this small city. At dusk, armadillos amble from their burrows, nosing around for insects to eat.

Whangarei, New Zealand. Quiet beaches on this tiny island are popular with both sailors and shellfish. Crabs scuttle through the warm sands while starfish and barnacles cling to rocks.

Whangarei is the antipode of...

Tangier, Morocco. The markets of this bustling city are always busy. Stray cats stroll around, popular with tourists and residents alike — but not with the local mice.

Yasawa, Fiji. Tropical seas surround this group of islands in the South Pacific Ocean. Squid swim through the warm waves, feasting on tiny fish. Yasawa is the antipode to...

Timbuktu, Mali. This famous city in west Africa is well known to explorers for its ancient libraries. The local goats travel long distances over scorching sands to find a place to graze.

The South Pole. You've arrived back at the poles! Under the southern lights, penguins huddle together on snowy slopes to stay warm at night.

The South Pole is the antipode of...

The North Pole. Daytime is hunting time for hungry polar bears. They use their massive claws to grab fish from the water and are excellent swimmers.

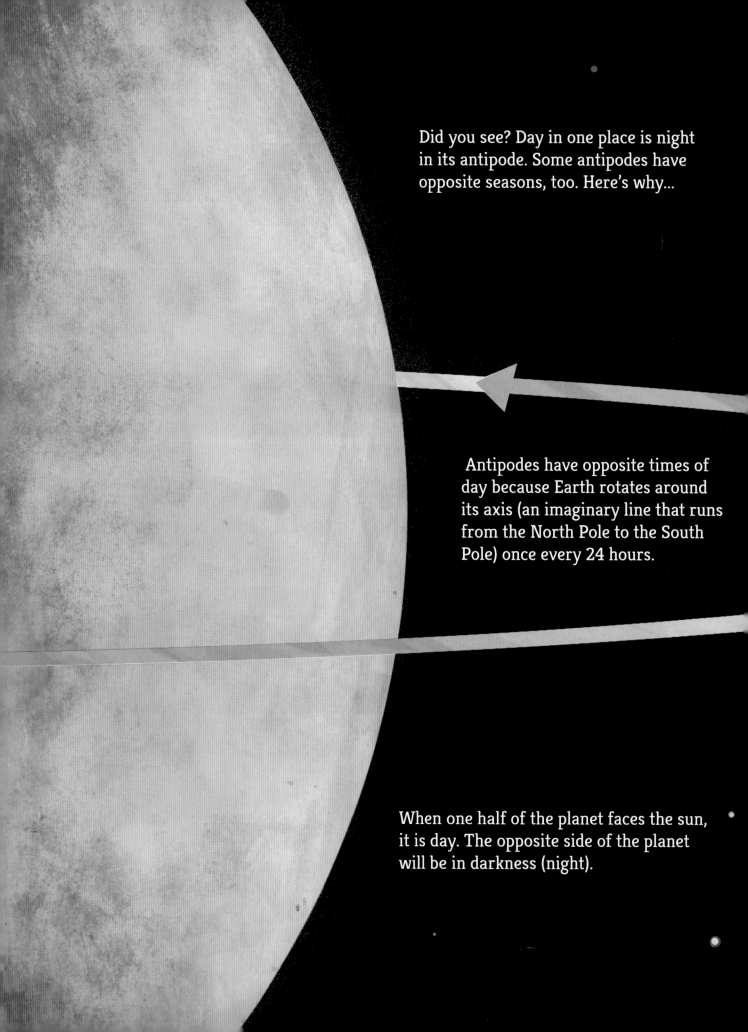

Did you see? Day in one place is night in its antipode. Some antipodes have opposite seasons, too. Here's why...

Antipodes have opposite times of day because Earth rotates around its axis (an imaginary line that runs from the North Pole to the South Pole) once every 24 hours.

When one half of the planet faces the sun, it is day. The opposite side of the planet will be in darkness (night).

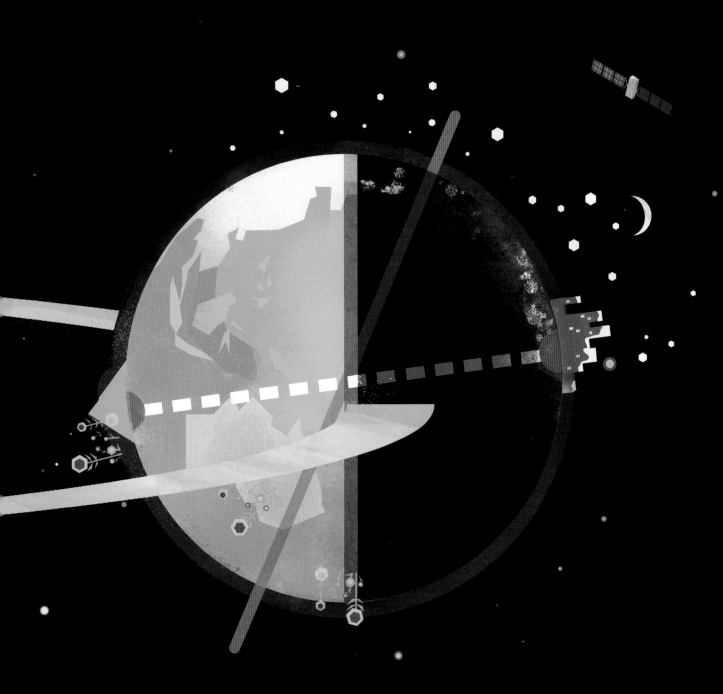

Since antipodes are opposite each
other, when one of them is in daylight,
it will be nighttime for the other.

Antipodes have opposite seasons because Earth orbits the sun at a permanent angle. This is called axial tilt.

Earth is divided into the Southern Hemisphere and the Northern Hemisphere.

As Earth orbits the sun, one hemisphere will be angled towards the sun, getting more direct sunlight. This makes it warmer (summer). The opposite side gets less direct sunlight which makes it colder (winter).

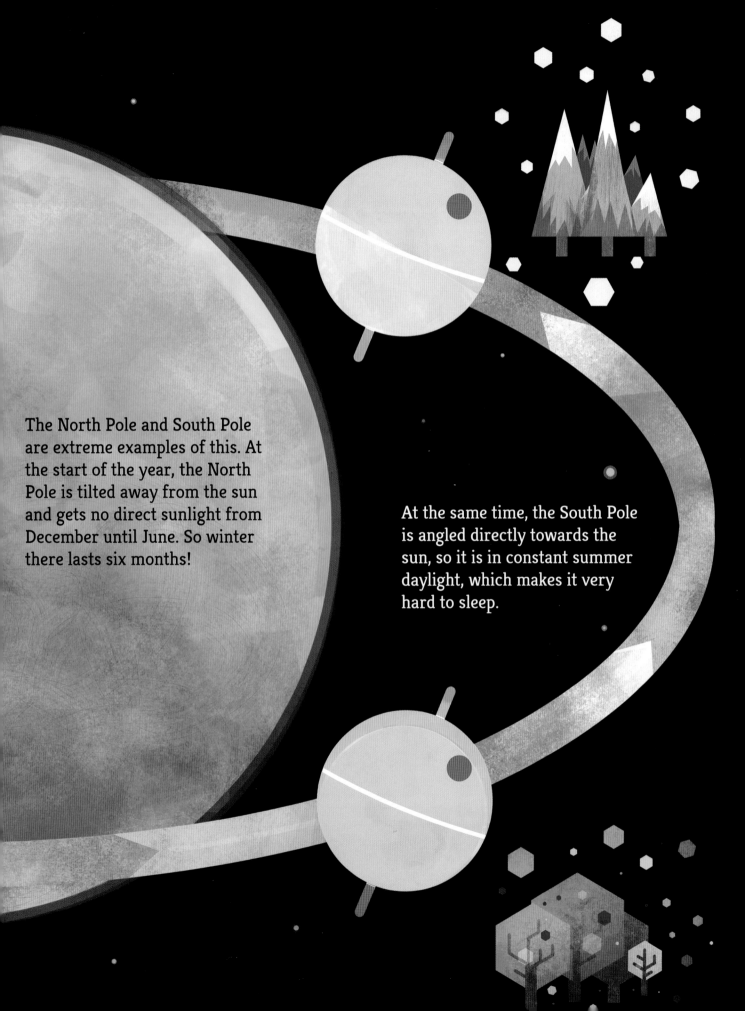

The North Pole and South Pole are extreme examples of this. At the start of the year, the North Pole is tilted away from the sun and gets no direct sunlight from December until June. So winter there lasts six months!

At the same time, the South Pole is angled directly towards the sun, so it is in constant summer daylight, which makes it very hard to sleep.

How would you find your antipode?

Find your home on a globe and see
what lies directly opposite it.

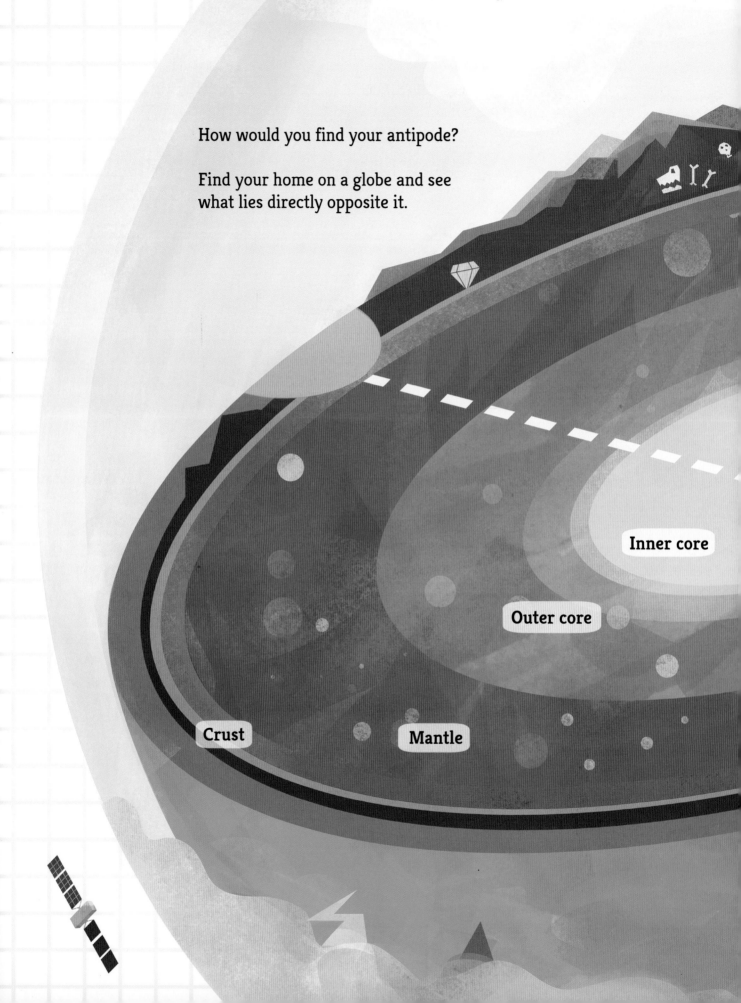

Inner core

Outer core

Crust

Mantle

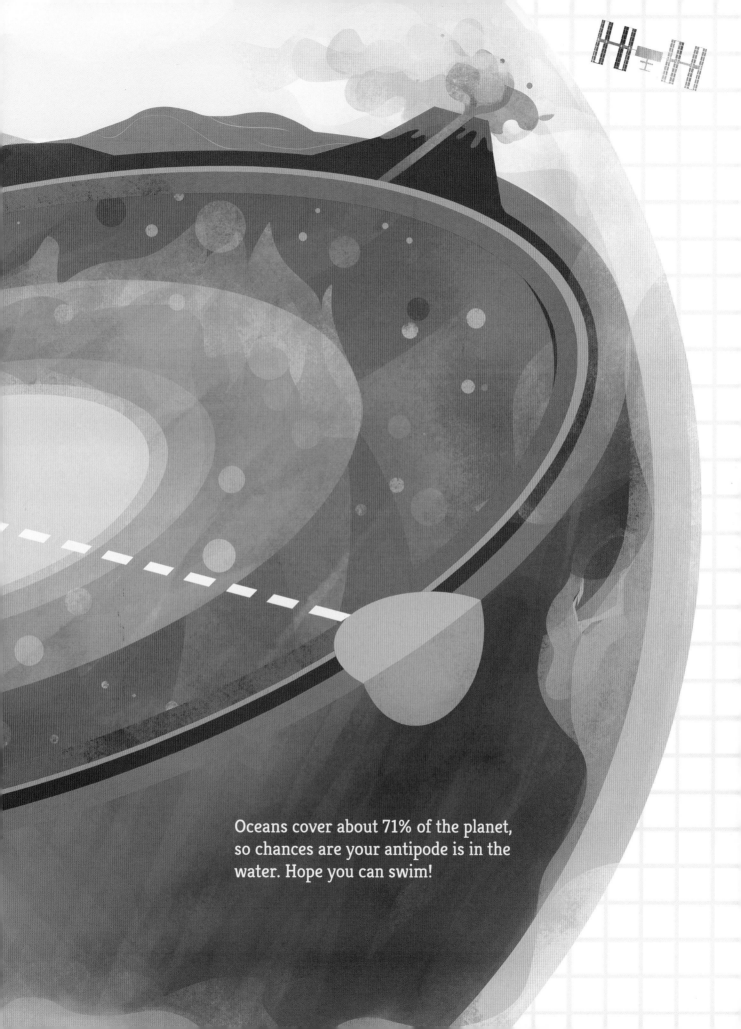

Oceans cover about 71% of the planet, so chances are your antipode is in the water. Hope you can swim!

GIANT PANDA
(Ailuropoda melanoleuca)
Xi'an

COASTAL COPPER BUTTERFLY
(Lycaena salustius)
Whangarei

HOUSE MOUSE
(Mus musculus)
Tangeir

LANTERN BUG
(Pyrops candelaria)
Kaoh Nheaek

OCHRE STARFISH
a.k.a PURPLE
SEA STAR
(Pisaster ochraceus)
Whangarei

JAPANESE PIPISTRELLE
a.k.a JAPANESE HOUSE BAT
(Pipistrellus abramus)
Hong Kong

MACARONI PENGUIN
(Eudyptes chrysolophus)
South Pole

SOOTY TERN a.k.a MANUTARA
(Onychoprion fuscatus)
Easter Island

PILOT FISH
(Naucrates ductor)
Yasawa

POLAR BEAR
(Ursus maritimus)
North Pole

SAHELIAN GOAT
(Capra aegagrus hircus)
Timbuktu

HORSE
(Equus ferus caballus)
Easter Island

CAT
(Felis catus)
Tangeir

SOUTH AMERICAN
GRAY FOX a.k.a CHILLA
(Lycalopex griseus)
Monte Sarmiento

WOLF SNAKE
(Lycodon Zoosvictoriae)
Kaoh Nheaek

GENTOO PENGUIN
(Pygoscelis Papua)
South Pole

TIGER SHARK
(Galeocerdo cuvier)
Yasawa

GREAT INDIAN BUSTARD
(Ardeotis nigriceps)
Desert National Park

GOLOMYANKA
(Comephorus baikalensis)
Lake Baikal

GREEN TURTLE
(Chelonia mydas)
The Big Island

OWLET MOTH
(Peridrome orbicularis)
Kaoh Nheaek

DESERT HEDGEHOG
(Paraechinus aethiopicus)
Timbuktu

ARCTIC COD
(Arctogadus glacialis)
North Pole

MONARD'S DROPWING
(Trithemis Monardi)
Okavango Delta

MAGNIFICENT FRIGATEBIRD
(Fregata magnificens)
Easter Island